PREFACE

In 1995, RAND published a report exploring the feasibility and societal implications of providing "universal" access to electronic mail within the United States (Robert H. Anderson et al., *Universal Access to E-Mail: Feasibility and Societal Implications,* MR-650-MF). Among its major policy conclusions and recommendations in that report were these:

- It is critical that electronic mail be a basic service in a National Information Infrastructure.
- There are no fundamental technical barriers to providing universal access to electronic mail services.
- It is important to reduce the increasing gaps in access to basic electronic information services, specifically, access to electronic mail services.

Analyses of Current Population Survey data for the report indicated that, even as computer and Internet use had grown dramatically, access gaps had widened rather than narrowed in the United States since the 1980s.

The sponsor of that study, the John and Mary R. Markle Foundation, supported a subsequent study on a related subject of which this report is a part. Here, we use Current Population Survey data from 1997 to update the trends in computers and connectivity that were highlighted in the 1995 report.

We expect these analyses to be of interest to government agencies exploring the feasibility of providing services to citizens via electronic communication, to organizations and individuals interested in expanding on-line usage to those currently without such access, and to policymakers attempting to understand and shape—or at least ameliorate—the social impacts of the continuing information revolution.

This research was performed under the auspices of RAND's Science and Technology unit, directed by Stephen Rattien. For further information on this report, please contact the authors (Tora_Bikson@rand.org, Stan_Panis@rand.org). For an account of the complete study of which this research is a part, please see *Sending Your Government a Message: E-Mail Communications Between Citizens and Government* (RAND, MR-1095-MF, 1999), by C. R. Neu, Robert H. Anderson, and Tora K. Bikson.

Citizens, Computers, and Connectivity

A Review of Trends

Tora K. Bikson • Constantijn W. A. Panis

Supported by the John and Mary R. Markle Foundation

RAND
Science and Technology

CONTENTS

Preface iii

Figures vii

Tables ix

Acknowledgments xi

Abbreviations xiii

CITIZENS, COMPUTERS, AND CONNECTIVITY: A REVIEW OF TRENDS 1

- Reviewing Current Trends 3
  - Approach to the CPS Data 4
  - Results of Data Analysis 9
- Conclusions 28

Appendix

ADDITIONAL INFORMATION ON CITIZENS, COMPUTERS, AND CONNECTIVITY 31

References 43

FIGURES

1. Growth in Internet Hosts, 1993–1998 2
2. U.S. Census/CPS Data 6
3. People in Computer Households, by Income 10
4. People Using Network Services, by Income 10
5. People in Computer Households, by Education 14
6. People Using Network Services, by Education 14
7. People in Computer Households, by Race/Ethnicity . . 18
8. People Using Network Services, by Race/Ethnicity . . . 18
9. People in Computer Households, by Age 21
10. People Using Network Services, by Age 21
11. People in Computer Households, by Gender 24
12. People Using Network Services, by Gender 24
13. People in Computer Households, by Location 26
14. People Using Network Services, by Location 26

A.1. Stylized Home Computer Penetration Between 1993 and 1997, by Income Quartile 36

TABLES

1. Summary of Socioeconomic Findings 29
A.1. Logit Estimates 33
A.2. Gross and Net Percentages of People Who Have Access to a Home Computer and Use Network Services at Home or Work 35
A.3. Computer Use at Home 38

ACKNOWLEDGMENTS

We are grateful to Lloyd N. Morrisett, President of the Markle Foundation at the time this work was begun, and to Zoe Baird, his successor, for their support and counsel throughout this project.

Bruce C. Vladeck, Administrator of HCFA at the time this study was begun, generously gave us permission to pursue our case study of HCFA's communications with Medicare beneficiaries. Joyce Somsak and Megan Arts of the HCFA staff were instrumental in guiding us to the many other staff members who patiently and clearly explained the workings of the Medicare program and the vast flow of communications related to it. Staff members at ten HCFA contractors also shared with us their procedures for managing the Medicare program on a day-to-day basis. We are grateful to all of them.

At California EDD, our request to identify and explore areas of individualized communications for potential case study purposes met with a positive response from Josetta Bull, Deputy Director, Information Technology Branch, and Deborah Bronow, Assistant Deputy Director, Unemployment Insurance Division. They facilitated meetings and made contacts for us with appropriate individuals throughout the department. We are especially grateful to Talbott Smith, Chief of the Administrative, Workforce and Enterprise Solutions Section in the Information Systems Division, and to Gretchen Jung, then Chief of the Oversight, Data and Support Section of the Unemployment Insurance Division, for giving us considerable amounts of their time and attention, providing us with needed data and documentation, and helping us to schedule appointments with representatives of other units over numerous visits to EDD. We appreciate as well the cooperation of the many other EDD unit representatives without whose assistance we could not have completed the case study.

Staff at other government agencies also offered insights into the potential for greater use of e-mail and the potential pitfalls that lie along the way. Especially helpful were Leo Campbell of the United States Postal Service and John Sabo of the Social Security Administration.

Among our RAND colleagues, Joanna Heilbrunn provided invaluable assistance, collecting much of the information for the HCFA case study and interviewing HCFA contractors. Maria Sanchez did much of the basic work that led to our survey of current government use of e-mail and the Internet. Ashin Rastegar assisted with the analysis of access to e-mail.

Finally, we are indebted to Ingo Vogelsang of the Boston University Economics Department, Lee S. Sproull of the Boston University School of Management, and Norman G. Litell, Director of Corporate Risk Management at Visa U.S.A., Inc., for insightful and constructive reviews of early drafts of this report.

Any errors in fact or judgment that remain in this report despite the efforts of all those noted above are, of course, our responsibility.

ABBREVIATIONS

ANOVA	analysis of variance
CPS	Current Population Survey
EDD	Employment Development Department
ETS	Educational Testing Service
HCFA	Health Care Financing Administration
OLS	Ordinary Least Squares
PC	personal computer

CITIZENS, COMPUTERS, AND CONNECTIVITY: A REVIEW OF TRENDS

As each new medium of communion has emerged, "its proponents have pointed out its value not only to the owners and early users, but to the broader society as well" (Firestone and Garner, 1998, pp. v–xi). In this respect, digital communication media do not differ from their predecessors. The Clinton/Gore administration, for example, announced expectations that the Internet would serve as a vehicle to "reinvent government" and "transform society" (National Partnership for Reinventing Government, 1993). And, according to a recent National Research Council report, computing and communication technologies and associated enterprises had advanced enough by the early 1990s "to be accepted as public infrastructure" (National Research Council, Computer Science and Telecommunications Board, 1997a, pp. 1–6).

Not surprisingly, the strategic plans of many government agencies assume the widespread availability of such an infrastructure. The Office of Management and Budget, for instance, expects that "75 percent of all transactions between individuals and the government—including such services as delivery of food stamps, Social Security benefits, and Medicaid information—will take place electronically" (The Benton Foundation, 1998, pp. 1–8). But are these aims realizable?

Our case studies of two agencies (see Chapters Three and Four of *Sending Your Government a Message*) suggest that e-mail could be used to handle individualized communications between government services and their citizen clients in ways that would potentially yield both cost savings and quality improvements. Chapter Five of that report reviews key technical and institutional barriers to making the national information infrastructure useful for the conduct of such official interactions. Here we examine trends in accessibility of computers and networked digital media to the government's clients.

At an aggregate level, the continuing rapid expansion of the electronic communication infrastructure is unquestionable (see Figure 1). A 1995 RAND report cited the number of Internet host machines in that year as over 6.7 million; by now, that number exceeds 30 million (Anderson et al., 1995). Internet traffic continues to grow at a dramatic rate as well, reportedly doubling every six to nine months (National Research Council, Computer Science and Telecommunications Board, 1997b, pp. 7–9). Further, among current Internet users who responded to a Forrester Research Inc. survey, the most common network activity by far is e-mail, reported by over 88 percent of households that had been on-line at least three times in the previous three months.[1]

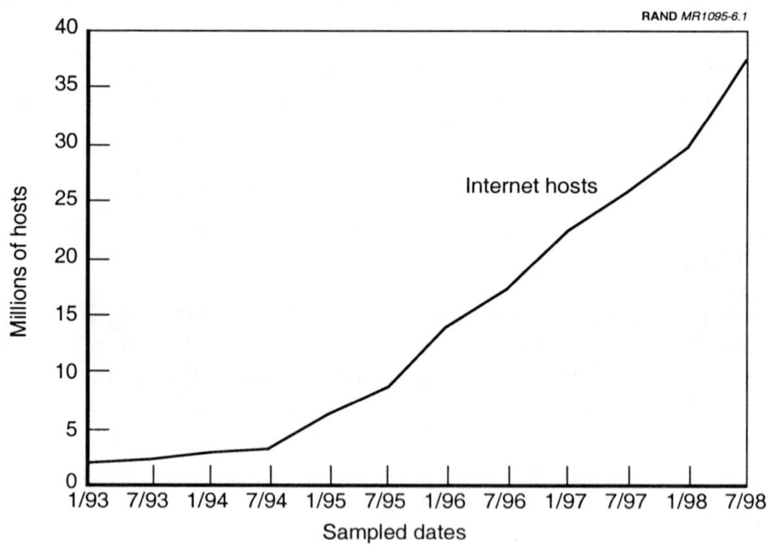

Figure 1—Growth in Internet Hosts, 1993–1998

[1]"Entertainment Technology," *Wall Street Journal*, March 22, 1999. This special section presents results of a survey of 100,000 North American households with both computers and network access.

While encouraging, such aggregate statistics do not provide a picture of how evenly computer and communication technologies are distributed over the country's varied demographic constituencies. "Looming large," for instance, "is the concern that the Internet may be accessible only to the most affluent and educated members of our society," according to a recent article in *Science* (Hoffman and Novak, 1998). Future policies for governmental and societal uses of these advanced media will be critically affected by the breadth and equity of their reach.

As we argued in our earlier report (Anderson et al., 1995), the societal advantages of a networked information and communication infrastructure cannot be fully realized until there is approximately universal service.[2] For this, it is important to provide an updated understanding of trends in citizen access to computers and networks in the United States.

REVIEWING CURRENT TRENDS

In this report, we present a detailed review of trends in access to computers and communication networks in the U.S. population. The review parallels and updates trends discussed in our earlier report (Anderson et al., 1995). Here, however, we include data from the October 1997 Current Population Survey (CPS), along with data gathered from similar surveys in October of 1993, 1989, and 1984 (U.S. Bureau of the Census, 1998, 1994, 1990, and 1985).

The CPS is a large-scale random-sample survey of households conducted monthly by the Bureau of the Census. It is the source for much of the official data published by the Bureau of Labor Statistics. The Bureau of the Census periodically adds supplements to the CPS base questionnaires to gain more insight into topics of interest. In this review, as in the earlier study, we chose supplements for examination that include comparable questions on computer use by each individual in a household. However, since the 1984 questions are not always comparable to those asked in later years, we rely chiefly on

---

[2]See also National Research Council, Computer Science and Telecommunications Board, 1997b, pp. 29–31.

data from the more recent surveys, examining 1984 data only in relation to the availability of a personal computer in the household.[3]

Approach to the CPS Data

CPS data are suitable for analysis at the household or individual level. Our study treats the individual as the unit of analysis. Although some outcomes of interest (e.g., presence of a computer at home) are readily interpretable at either level, others (especially behavioral variables, such as use of networked services) are not. However, where both levels of analysis are appropriate, patterns of findings at the individual and household levels do not differ.

At the individual level, the statistical analyses we describe below are based in the main on 266,378 observations (123,249 in 1997 and 143,129 in 1993); some figures and tables also represent data from 1989 and 1984 (based on 146,850 and 151,832 observations, respectively). In every year, the sample comprises noninstitutionalized civilians in the United States living in households. Both adults and children are in the sample.[4] The analyses were done using individual weights that approximately equal the inverse of the probability of being in the sample, adjusted for interview response rates and normalized to add up to the sample size.

Outcome variables. To represent access to information and communication technology, we employ two binary outcome variables defined as they were in our earlier report (Anderson et al., 1995, pp. 20–21). One, access to a computer at home, is a single-item measure; it receives a positive value if there is a computer in an individual's household. At this level of analysis, penetration of computers refers to the percentage of individuals with household access (rather than the percentage of households that have computers). Strictly speaking, we measure presence of a computer in the household irrespective of ownership. We assume that all household members have access to a computer present in the household.

---

[3]Most notably, the 1984 CPS did not solicit information about use of e-mail or other network-based activity.

[4]Questions about computer and network use are asked only in reference to persons 3 years or older.

The other outcome variable, use of network services, represents use of a computer either at home or at work to connect to an electronic network. A derived measure, this variable receives a positive value if an individual uses a computer in any one of the following ways:

- At home to connect to bulletin boards;
- At home to connect to a computer at work;
- At work for communications (seen as distinct from word processing, desktop publishing, newsletter creation, and so on);
- At home or at work for e-mail.

It is important to include connectivity in the workplace as well as from home in the definition because it provides a more complete picture of the degree to which individuals use electronic avenues to communicate with others. In 1997, more individuals reported using network services at home (15 percent) than at work (13 percent); this contrasts with data obtained in 1993, when workplace users still outnumbered home users. However, as before, there is considerable overlap among them. For example, over 40 percent of those who access a network from their workplace also do so from home.[5] Overall trends for the two outcome variables are shown in Figure 2. The penetration of home computers increased from 18 percent in 1989 to 27 percent in 1993 and 42 percent in 1997. Moreover, by 1997 about a quarter of the people in computerized households had access to two or more computers there.[6] The use of network services from either home or work increased from 6 percent in 1989 to 11 percent in 1993 and 23 percent in 1997. Among those with a home computer, however, 42 percent reported use of network services in 1997.

---

[5]The CPS does not directly obtain information about the nature of network use for individualized communication from schools and libraries. It is important to note that access to the Web does not necessarily imply access to an e-mail account (and vice versa). If responses indicating school-based use (as reported by parents) are added to the derived variable representing network service use, the total number of network users increases by less than 1 percent (a statistically negligible amount), but an unhelpful ambiguity about the definition of network use is created. For these reasons, we did not include parents' reports of children's school-based use of a network in defining this outcome variable.

[6]In 1997, the CPS added a question asking how many computers there were if the initial question about the presence of a computer at home was answered positively.

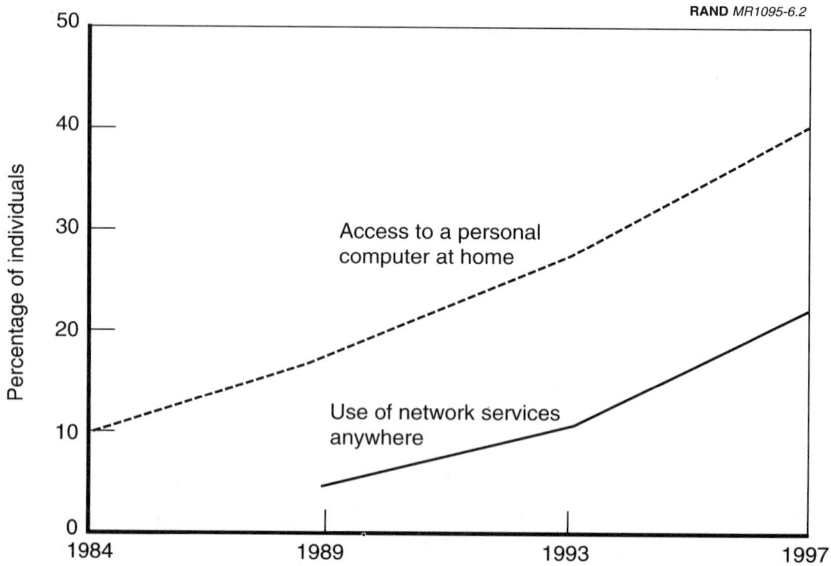

Figure 2—U.S. Census/CPS Data

Predictor variables. Six predictor variables constitute the core of our review of trends: income, education, race/ethnicity, age, sex, and location of residence.[7] Income, a categorical variable defined by quartiles, refers to the total income of the individual's household. Location, another variable defined at the household level, reflects whether the individual lives in an urban or a rural area. Remaining predictor variables refer only to the individual. Each explanatory variable is further described in our discussion of results, below.

Analysis plan. In investigating the CPS data, our goal was to learn whether and, if so, how socioeconomic characteristics are correlated with distribution patterns and diffusion trends in access to computers and digital networks. Figure 2 presents aggregated CPS data

---

[7]Our analyses are intended to be descriptive without taking a position on the direction of causality. It may be the case that the presence of a home computer makes someone more productive and thereby increases his or her income. We ignore such potential reverse causality and treat the socioeconomic characteristics as independent predictor variables.

representing the two outcome variables of interest for the U.S. population in 1997, 1993, and 1989 (and, for access to a computer at home, in 1984). The analysis was designed to answer two questions about these outcomes at the individual level:

- In 1997, in comparison to their proportion of the population, are any socioeconomically defined groups significantly underrepresented among those with computers at home and those who use network services anywhere?
- How have recent trends contributed to the present-day distribution of outcomes? That is, have differences between groups in access to computers and communication technology narrowed, remained constant, or widened over recent years?

Answers to these questions are tested statistically in several ways. First, we examined differences in access to a computer at home and use of network services across socioeconomic groups separately for each year for which data are available. These differences, generated by cross-tabulations, are shown in graphs of trends for each socioeconomic variable of interest. Because of very large sample sizes, comparisons between groups for all socioeconomic dimensions and for each year of study are generally statistically significant; when they are not, we explicitly note the absence of difference.[8]

For purposes of policy analysis and intervention, however, these "gross" differences may be misleading. Socioeconomic status variables are likely to be intercorrelated, meaning that an effort to investigate any one of them should control for the potential influence of the others.[9] Therefore, we also held constant the other predictor

---

[8]Statistical significance is determined here on the basis of the Pearson chi-square test. Note that all weights are normalized to add up to the sample size.

[9]For example, suppose it is a policy goal to provide equal use of network services across socioeconomic groups. As we show below, black individuals tend to use network services to a lesser extent than whites. This may prompt policymakers to direct efforts to increase use of network services to black communities. However, as we also show, low-income individuals likewise tend to make less use of network services than do high-income individuals. And because the average household income among blacks is lower than among whites, it may be the case that part or all of the racial/ethnic difference is due to income differentials. More-equal use of network services across socioeconomic groups, then, might be achieved more effectively by targeting poor communities generally rather than black communities specifically.

variables studied, in order to recalculate the cross-tabulations based on such "net" percentages. Net figures can be interpreted as representing differences between individuals in access to computers and use of networks based on one socioeconomic dimension only, with otherwise equal characteristics. The same general pattern of findings emerges from the net data as from the unadjusted data, but net differences generally tend to be smaller.

Finally, we were interested in whether the gaps between socioeconomic groups narrowed, stayed the same, or widened between 1993 and 1997. There are several ways to measure changes in penetration gaps. Consider the discrepancy in access to a home computer between individuals in the bottom and top income quartiles. As we show below, 7 percent of individuals in the bottom income quartile and 55 percent of those in the top income quartile had a home computer in 1993; by 1997, these penetration rates had grown to 15 and 75 percent, respectively. At the gross level, the income-based gap was 48 percentage points in 1993 and widened to 60 percentage points in 1997. However, adoption of new technologies tends to be fairly slow at low penetration levels, faster thereafter, and slower again as it reaches saturation, so it is not immediately obvious that the lower incomes fell farther behind. An alternative measure is, for example, the period of time it will take the bottom quartile to achieve the same penetration rate as the top quartile enjoyed at the time of the survey. That is, how long will it take the bottom quartile to grow from its 1993 level of 7 percent to the 55 percent of the top quartile, and how long will it take to increase penetration from its 1997 level of 15 percent to the top quartile's 75 percent? Has the penetration lag lengthened, stayed the same, or shortened between 1993 and 1997?

The appendix explains in detail how we test for changes between 1993 and 1997 in such lags or gaps. We develop logit models of access to a home computer and use of network services based on pooled 1993 and 1997 data, and estimate the extent to which coefficients have changed between 1993 and 1997. The models are multivariate; that is, we test only for changes in "net" gaps (see Table A.1). The appendix also provides a table with both gross and net percentage data for the two outcome variables for 1989, 1993, and 1997 for purposes of comparison (see Table A.2).

The following discussion emphasizes gross results, but we systematically point out where and to what extent these results overstate disparities across socioeconomic groups.

Results of Data Analysis

In what follows, findings from the data analysis are presented separately for each of the six predictor variables.

Differences by household income. Figures 3 and 4 show, respectively, trend data representing the percentage of individuals reporting that there is a computer in the household and that they use network services, as a function of household income category. We distinguish four income categories, chosen such that each captures approximately 25 percent of the population. In 1997, the quartile cutoff income levels were $20,000, $35,000, and $60,000 per year.[10]

As is immediately clear in Figure 3, there are very large differences in household computer ownership across income categories. In 1997, about 15 percent of the lowest-income households had computers at home, whereas about 75 percent of the highest-earning quartile did. Four years earlier, the respective figures were around 7 percent and 55 percent. These data, then, continue to reflect highly significant differences in household computer access based on income.

The net disparities, controlling for the other key socioeconomic variables we studied, are not quite as large, but they remain substantial. For example, in 1997, on net, individuals in the top income quartile were over three times more likely than those in the bottom quartile to have access to a computer in the household (see the appendix, Table A.2). This net income-based gap is smaller than the gross figure, mostly because low-income individuals tend to have lower than average educational attainment. Specifically, about a third of

[10]Income quartile is based on total family income, i.e., the combined income of all family members aged 15+ during the past 12 months. (Households that did not provide an income figure are missing from our tabulations by income.) The CPS does not contain exact dollar figures; income is reported in 14 categories. We further collapsed those categories into four such that each contains roughly 25 percent of the respondents: Q1 (the bottom quartile) represents 26.1 percent; Q2, 22.5 percent; Q3, 26.3 percent; and Q4, 25.1 percent (all weighted).

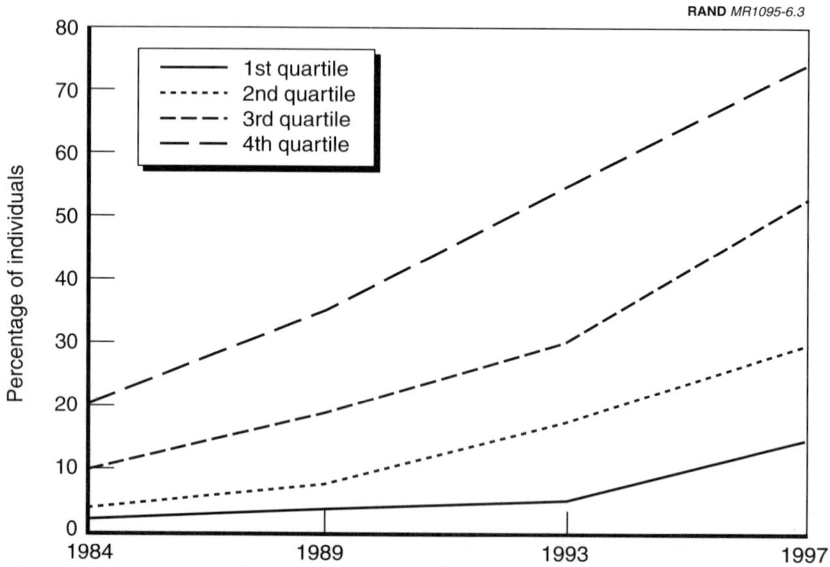

Figure 3—People in Computer Households, by Income

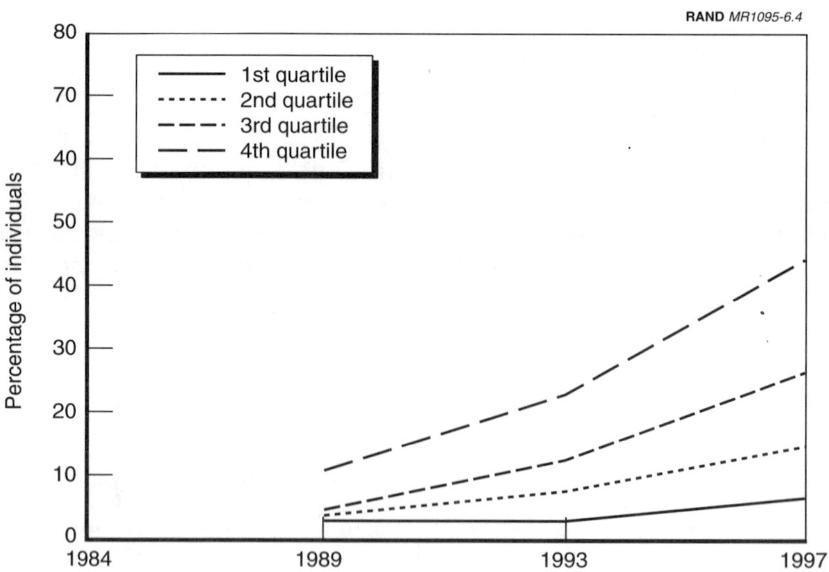

Figure 4—People Using Network Services, by Income

the income disparity is attributable to a concomitant effect from educational differences. These data thus continue to reflect highly significant differences in home computer access based on income.

Further, while the income-based gap in computer ownership was wide in 1993, it was even wider by 1997. Evidence for this finding comes from inspecting differences in percentages between the top and bottom quartiles in the two years: in 1993 these households differed by about 48 percent with respect to computer ownership; in 1997, the difference between these quartiles was about 60 percentage points. As explained above, such gross level gaps do not necessarily indicate that the bottom income quartile has fallen further behind. Our multivariate analysis of the change in the net discrepancy, however, indicates that the income-based gap did indeed widen somewhat between 1993 and 1997 (see appendix, Tables A.1 and A.2).

Although the extent of network service use either at home or at work is far less than the extent of household computer availability (see Figure 4), generally similar patterns appear for network use as a function of household income level.[11] Again, we find large differences between quartiles that tend to persist over time. In 1993, close to 3 percent of the lowest-income individuals used network services at home or work, whereas 23 percent of the highest income individuals used them. By 1997, these fractions had increased to 7 percent and about 45 percent, respectively. As before, conducting these same tests using net rather than gross figures yields somewhat smaller but still highly significant income-based differences in network service use.

Moreover, whether gross or net figures are used, differences in use of network services between the highest and lowest income groups have continued unabated. The trend lines, for example, show about a 20 percent difference in extent of network access between the top and bottom quartiles in 1993; by 1997, the gap between them has nearly doubled, to 38 percent (see also appendix Table A.2, to com-

---

[11]Recall that our measure of network use includes use at home or work but not at school, since the appropriate questions were not asked directly of students. This implies that we are likely to overstate differences in network use across income categories, because students who live away from their parents tend to have low household incomes.

pare net percentages). Statistical tests based on the prediction model plus assessments of how income and time interact with this outcome show that this gap in network use between individuals in the top and bottom income quartiles remained constant between 1993 and 1997 when other influences are controlled (see the appendix, Table A.1). The size of the gap between the bottom quartile and the third quartile also remained unchanged during those years while the gap between the second quartile and the bottom quartile decreased.

We thus conclude that there are large differences in both household computer ownership and use of network services across income categories. These differences are partly due to other socioeconomic characteristics, but they remain substantial even after controlling for those other characteristics. To help concretize these differences, the appendix presents a stylized penetration model (see Figure A.1). If the penetration rates for home computers keep increasing at the 1993–1997 pace, for example, then an individual in the bottom income quartile in 1997 could be expected to lag those in the top quartile by about nine years in obtaining access to a computer at home. If these same assumptions are applied to use of network services, the time lag for adoption of these new media between the bottom quartile and the top, other things being equal, is just over two years (see the appendix).

These results appear to be consistent with conclusions about income-based differences in access to computers and network service use reported in other recent studies (Katz and Aspden, 1996; Hoffman, Novak, and Venkatesh, 1998; National Telecommunications and Information Administration, 1998). Moreover, they provide partial support for the view that lack of a computer at home is a major barrier to network access among low-income groups. First, home computer gaps are larger than and growing more steadily than gaps in network access. Second, gaps in the use of network services are smaller in part because of access provided in the workplace, where individual employees do not have to pay for hardware and connectivity. However, it is usually employees in relatively higher level and better paid positions whose jobs are associated with e-mail use (Kreuger, 1993). Finally, there is clear agreement about there being considerable "churn" among Internet users, although estimated rates vary.[12] In any case, according to the national survey done by Katz and Aspden, "the key reported reason [why former users stopped using the Internet] was loss of access to a computer" (Katz and Aspden, 1996). It appears, then, that rapidly improving price/performance ratios for computers in recent years have not served to narrow (or even to hold constant) the digital divide.

Differences by educational attainment. Figures 5 and 6 show data for differences by educational attainment. Figure 5 presents household computer availability fractions for individuals without a high school diploma, for high school graduates, and for college graduates. (For purposes of this analysis, those still enrolled in primary school, secondary school, or undergraduate college were excluded from the dataset.) Persons with some college education, but without a bachelor's degree and not currently enrolled in a school, are included among high school graduates. As might be expected, there are large differences in household computer access by educational attainment.

Among persons without a high school diploma, only about 9 percent had a home computer in 1993. College graduates, by contrast, had a penetration rate of about 49 percent. All groups experienced an increase in home computers between 1993 and 1997, leading to penetration rates of about 17 percent and 66 percent in 1997 for those without a high school diploma and for college graduates, respectively. Controlling for other socioeconomic characteristics, the differences are substantially smaller but still highly significant statistically in both years (see net percentages in the appendix, Table A.2).

In the intervening four years, these education-based differences in access to household computers have held steady. That is, although

---

[12]The churn rate refers to the proportion of people who once used the Internet but have stopped using it, compared to the total number who have ever used it. Katz and Aspden (1996) estimate the churn rate at 50 percent, while Hoffman, Novak, and Venkatesh (1998) estimate it at 20 to 30 percent. The difference in estimates is a function of the length of the nonuse period set as the criterion for defining dropouts. Regardless of the criterion selected, the churn rate is substantial and warrants further investigation.

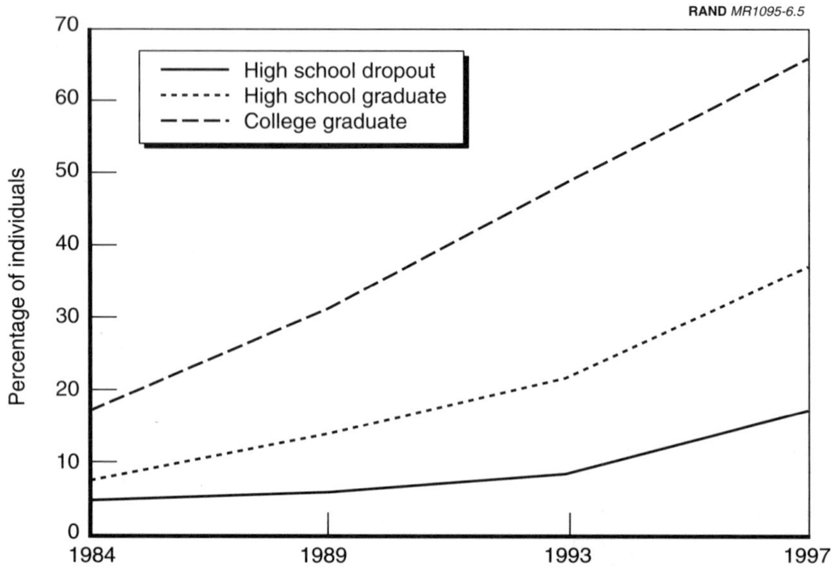

Figure 5—People in Computer Households, by Education

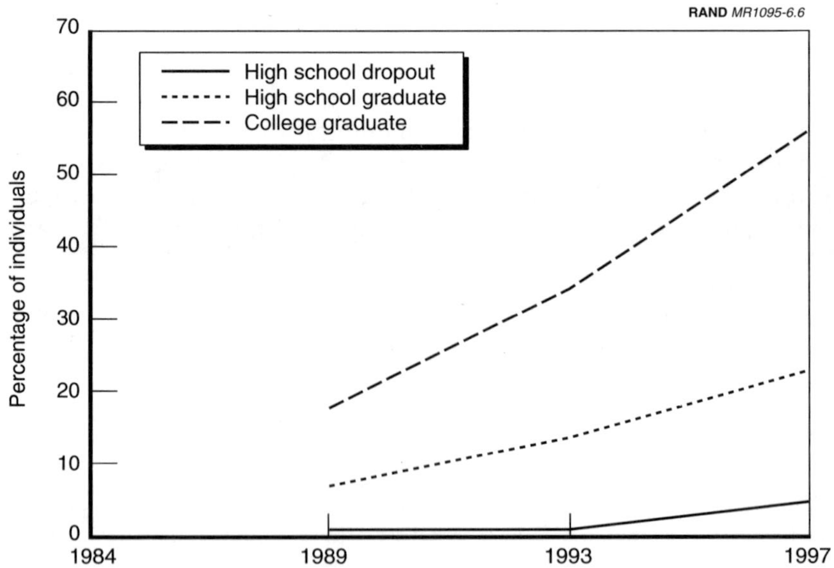

Figure 6—People Using Network Services, by Education

the gross percentage gap has widened between the upper and lower education levels, the increase, on net, is not statistically significant. These findings result both from the prediction equation we tested and from testing the significance of the interaction between year and education level as an influence on likelihood of having a home computer (see the appendix, Table A.1). Thus, the patterns of education-related differences are rather similar to but less sharp than the income-based differences in household computer access reported above.

Figure 6 shows the differences in network service use by education category. Not surprisingly, perhaps, we find that use of network services is strongly dominated by well-educated individuals. In 1993, just over 1 percent of individuals without high school diplomas used network services, compared to about 34 percent of college graduates. Both groups greatly increased their network use in 1997, to just over 5 percent and about 56 percent, respectively. As expected, the net differences are smaller than these but nonetheless significant (see the appendix, Table A.2).

Turning to the prediction equation, we learned that education-based gaps in use of network services between high school graduates and college graduates widened significantly from 1993 to 1997. This trend parallels the finding above related to income-based patterns of network use, where persistent or growing gaps are largely attributable to gains in access rates for the highest earning groups in those four years. It also parallels findings for education-based trends described in our 1995 report (Anderson et al., 1995), when increases in the network usage gap between 1989 and 1993 were largely explained by access growth for the most-educated group. By contrast, the size of the network access gap between high school dropouts and high school graduates actually narrowed between 1993 and 1997 (as did the network access gap between the bottom two income quartiles).

In summary, we find large differences in access to information and communication technology by educational attainment that are, with the notable exception of the narrowed gap in network use between high school dropouts and high school graduates, either holding steady or widening over time. Again, these results are consistent with findings from other national sample studies (Katz and Aspden,

1996; Hoffman, Kalsbeek, and Novak, 1996). Further, these education-based differences persist after accounting for income differences. Given the correlation between use of network services and knowledge of current political, professional, and organizational affairs described in the earlier report, these results suggest that disparities in access to network technologies may work to amplify differential knowledge produced by differing education levels alone.

Such differences are additionally problematic because of their potential influence on children's educational opportunities. If there is a computer at home, about 72 percent of those age 19 and younger will use it (see the appendix, Table A.3). Further, our review of the CPS children's questionnaire data indicates that, among students age 14 and younger, over 47 percent use the home computer specifically for educational programs (46.9 percent of boys and 49.5 percent of girls). These findings are consistent with other research showing few differences in patterns of children's computer use if access gaps based on parental income and education are overcome (Kraut et al., 1996).

Differences by race and ethnicity. Recent studies have raised concerns that African Americans and Hispanics are lagging behind in the use of digital media (Hoffman and Novak, 1998; Wilhelm, 1998). At least part of the race- and ethnicity-based difference is due to lower average household income and lower average educational attainment among these groups, as compared to non-Hispanic whites. However, our analysis shows that these characteristics do not account for the entire difference in outcome variables. Rather, racial and ethnic characteristics exert an independent and important influence on home computer access and network use.

For purposes of our analysis, we combine race and ethnicity to create a single variable with mutually exclusive categories. A five-level variable, it distinguishes Hispanics, non-Hispanic whites, non-Hispanic blacks, Native Americans (both Indians and Eskimos), and Americans of Asian descent (including Pacific Islanders). In subsequent comments, we refer to non-Hispanic whites as "whites" and to non-Hispanic blacks as "blacks." A small fraction of respondents are identified as "other" in the CPS data. We do not reflect the "other" category in the figures below (or in Table A.2 of the appendix); however, predictive models and tests based on those models take into account the influence of that category along with the defined race/ethnicity groups. Figures 7 and 8 portray the percentage of individuals with a computer in the household and access to network services at home or at work by racial/ethnic categories.

As Figure 7 reveals, the highest penetration rates for household computers are found among whites and Asians. In 1997, about 49 percent of whites and 56 percent of Asians lived in a household with a computer. Hispanics and blacks, by contrast, reported a penetration rate of around 22 percent, and Native Americans, 35 percent. A remarkable increase in home computer penetration is evident among Native Americans in the 1997 data.[13] As we mentioned, part of these differences may be due to average differences in other characteristics, notably household income and educational attainment.

Controlling for these characteristics, we nonetheless find substantial differences. That is, net of other influences, race/ethnicity has a statistically independent and sizable effect on household computer access (see the appendix, Table A.2). In particular, Hispanics and blacks are currently underrepresented among computerized households. Patterns of significant racial/ethnic difference in household computer access are also evident in the 1993 data. Since 1993, however, there have been some noteworthy changes in their relative size. Specifically, from 1993 to 1997 (when the influence of other socioeconomic variables is held constant), the household computer gap has widened significantly between blacks and Hispanics, on the one hand, and whites, on the other; has narrowed by a statistically significant margin between Native Americans and whites; and remains unchanged between Asian Americans and whites (see the appendix, Table A.1).

It should, however, be underscored that the discrepancy between racial and ethnic groups is fairly small at the higher income levels. Home computer penetration among Hispanics in the top income quartile is 75 percent, not much below the rates for non-Hispanic whites (83 percent) and Asians (87 percent). Penetration rates for

---

[13]Native Americans are oversampled in the CPS. In 1993, 1,703 Native Americans were interviewed; in 1997, there were 1,763. By contrast, the Nielsen Internet Demographic Study (IDS) bases its 1996–1997 results on a sample that includes only 75 Native American respondents. See Hoffman, Novak, and Venkatesh, 1998, for a discussion of this and other issues involved in using Nielsen IDS data to make inferences about racial and ethnic differences in technology use.

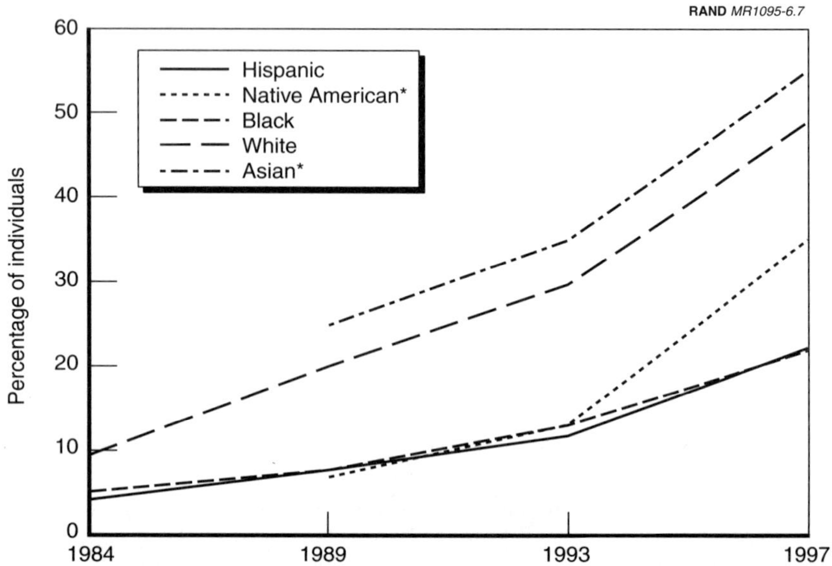

*No data available for these groups in 1984.

Figure 7—People in Computer Households, by Race/Ethnicity

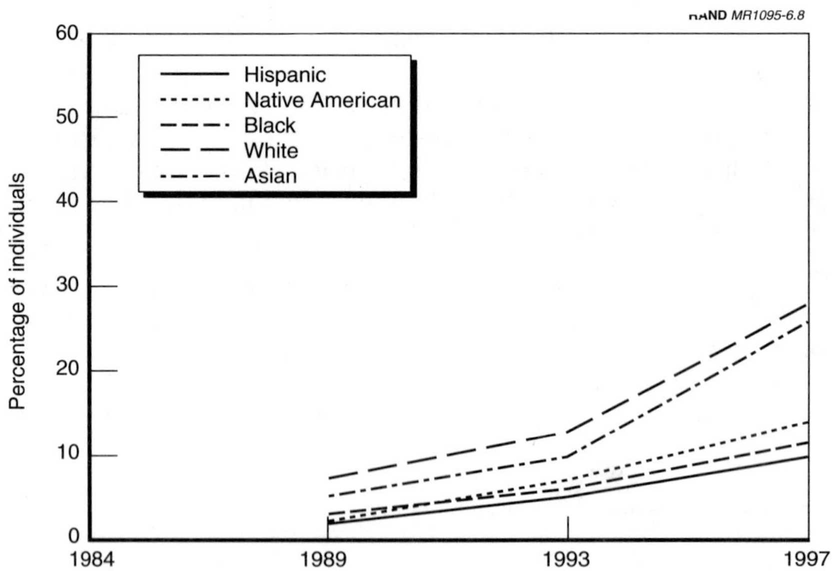

Figure 8—People Using Network Services, by Race/Ethnicity

blacks and Native Americans in the top income quartile are 66 and 79 percent, respectively.

Differential use of network services as a function of race/ethnicity is apparent in Figure 8. Again there are significant between-group differences, even when the influence of other socioeconomic characteristics is controlled. Net differences are also somewhat smaller than those observed for household computer access (see the appendix, Table A.3), as expected. An examination of changes in gaps between 1993 and 1997, however, shows some surprising results.

In 1993, for instance, Asian Americans had the lowest net rate of network service use even though they had the highest net rate of household computer ownership among the racial/ethnic groups we studied. By 1997, the gap in network service use rates between this group and the highest penetration group (whites) had narrowed significantly, controlling for the influence of other socioeconomic variables; and it can be expected to close in the near future. In marked contrast, the gaps in network service use between blacks and Hispanics versus socioeconomically similar whites widened significantly between 1993 and 1997, after having remained stable during the previous four years. For Native Americans, despite their substantial net gain in access to computers at home, the gap between them and socioeconomically similar whites in network service use remained constant from 1993 to 1997.

On the whole, then, we find rather large and persistent differences across race/ethnicity in both the availability of a household computer and the use of network services when the influence of other socioeconomic variables is controlled. These findings are consistent with results from other research on ethnic and racial gaps in access to digital media (National Telecommunications and Information Administration, 1998; Hoffman, Novak, and Venkatesh, 1998; Kraut et al., 1996). For instance, Hoffman and her colleagues point out that Asian Americans and Native Americans are—in net terms—among the most "wired" demographic groups, while African Americans and Hispanics are the least connected. The HomeNet study carried out by Kraut and his colleagues likewise finds race/ethnicity differences in technology use not explained by variation in income or education.

As we pointed out in our earlier report, we had not expected to find race/ethnicity differences in computer access and connectivity that were not attributable to variation in income, education, or other demographic characteristics. The size and endurance of the differences, however, indicate that race/ethnicity gaps deserve further investigation.

Differences by age. We now turn to differences by age.[14] In the figures that follow, for individuals between the ages of 20 and 60, we break down information about household computer access and network service use by decade. For analytic purposes, however, we rely on four categories, distinguishing between individuals under 20 years of age, between 20 and 39, between 40 and 59, and 60 years of age and older (preserving comparability with our earlier study). Boundaries based on age are admittedly arbitrary, and different studies employ different cutoffs and/or different numbers of categories. Particular boundary choices do not, however, appear to influence analytic results in ways that would affect most policy decisions.[15]

Figures 9 and 10 show age-related data on computer access and connectivity. As Figure 9 suggests, availability of a home computer is not marked by wide divisions between age-defined categories until about age 60, when rates of access to a household computer decline steeply. In 1997, around 40 to 50 percent of all individuals under age 60 had access to a home computer, whereas only about 20 percent of individuals above age 60 lived in a household with a computer. Even when other socioeconomic variables are controlled, this difference is

---

[14]The treatment of age is determined by the objectives of the study. The decision to purchase a computer is in part influenced by the size and composition of a household. However, our aim is to document socioeconomic and demographic differences in access to information and communication technology, rather than differences in personal ownership or use. The connection between presence of a computer at home and access to it requires only the relatively plausible assumption that the computer is available to all household members.

[15]In our exploratory analyses, we distinguished as many as eight different age categories. In Figures 6.9 and 6.10, we have retained six categories to permit inspection of outcome trends for individuals who are going to reach Medicare-eligible age levels in the relatively near term (see Chapter Three of *Sending Your Government a Message*). However, for analysis purposes, we collapsed them into the four categories presented here and employed in our previous study, because the patterns that emerged were robust to this more parsimonious classification.

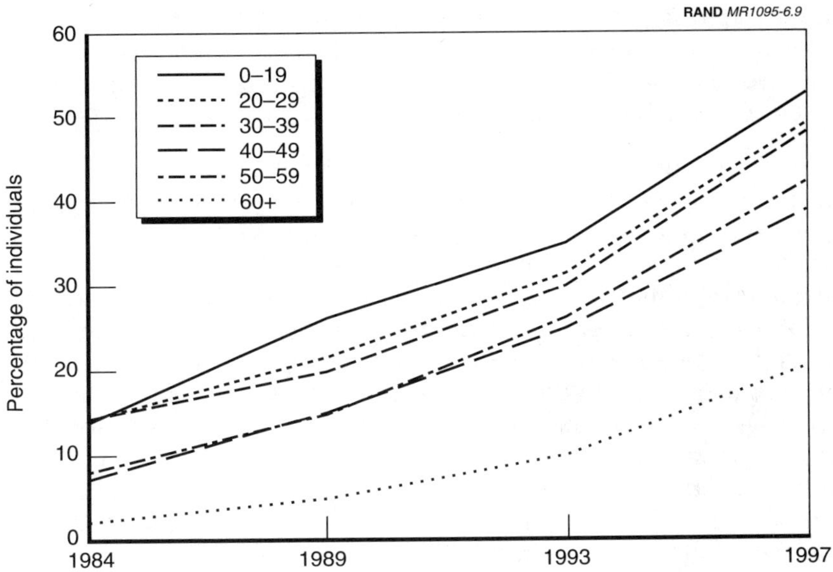

Figure 9—People in Computer Households, by Age

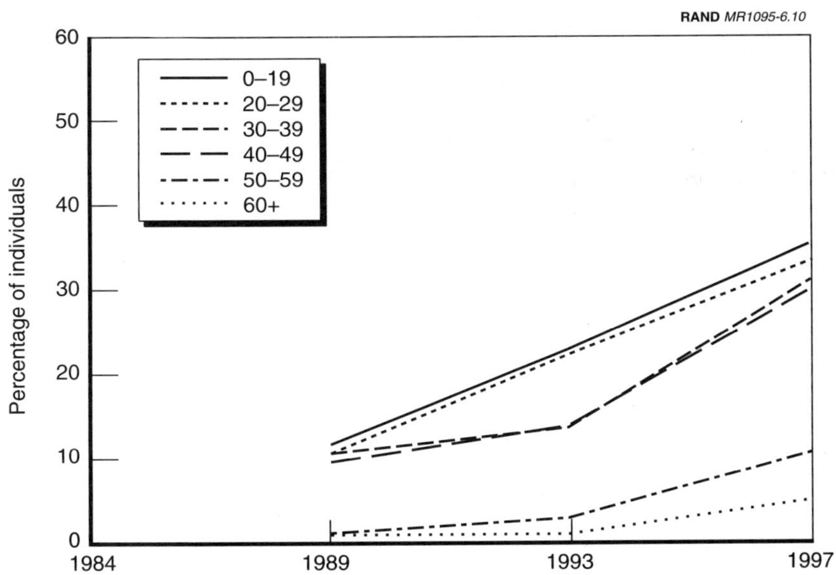

Figure 10—People Using Network Services, by Age

highly significant (see the appendix, Table A.1). Moreover, while age-based gaps have remained essentially constant across the other age groups since 1993, the gap in home computer ownership for the over-60 group has increased significantly (Table A.2).

Figure 10 additionally reveals the existence of large differences in the use of network services across the age categories defined. Gross percentages suggest disparities at both ends of the age range, even though the youngest group overtook the oldest. In 1997, about 7 percent of all individuals age 60 and older, and about 11 percent of all individuals under age 20, reportedly used network services; these figures compare with over 33 percent of all people between the ages of 20 and 59 who used network services. However, these figures are quite different from net percentages that control for other socioeconomic variables (see the appendix, Table A.2). When other characteristics are controlled, the gap between younger individuals and those age 20 to 59 in use of network services is substantially decreased. Older adults, in contrast, make markedly less use of network services than any other age group, and the difference remains large and significant even after the influence of other socioeconomic variables is controlled. Further, the gaps in network use between all individuals over age 40 and their demographically similar counterparts in the younger adult age group (20 to 39) has increased substantially from 1993 to 1997.

As we noted earlier, it is possible that the measure of network use employed here underrepresents students' access to on-line services, because no CPS questions directly addressed network use at school. However, recent careful studies of wired schools indicate that even where computers and connectivity are available, there is very little network service use on the part of students at school (Schofield, 1995; Schofield and Davidson, 1997). Moreover, these technologies tend to be largely available in schools attended by students from higher-income households who also have access at home. A recent Educational Testing Service (ETS) study concluded that minority and poor students had significantly less access to computers in their classes than did more-affluent children. Further, schools with a predominantly minority enrollment had an average student-computer ratio of 17 to 1, compared with the national average of 10 to 1; for computers with advanced graphics or interactive video, the discrepancies were even larger (Educational Testing Service, 1997).

These conclusions are corroborated, in part, by the detailed comparative study of Internet and Web use among black and white students carried out by Hoffman, Novak, and Venkatesh (1998). Their research found very large gaps in use of those technologies as a function of ethnicity; the difference was attributable to black students' relative lack of access to the Internet and Web outside of school, and especially to the lack of a home computer. A Yankelovich Monitor study similarly concludes that "what bars entry to cyberspace among African Americans" is not owning a home PC.[16]

We believe, then, that there have been substantial gains in connectivity for those at the lower end of the age range, but that the wiring of K–12 schools is probably not implicated in this trend. Rather, increased computer and network access at home probably accounts for this major change. In contrast, optimistic expectations for near-term connectivity gains among those over 60 (see Anderson et al., 1995) are disconfirmed by analyses of the 1997 data.

Differences by sex. Unlike our analyses based on the preceding socioeconomic variables, our analyses based on sex find little variation in access to home computers and use of network services, as Figures 11 and 12 illustrate. While the gross data shown in Figure 11 suggest a 2.5 percent discrepancy in rate of access to a computer at home in 1997, that gender difference disappears entirely when the influence of other socioeconomic variables is controlled (see the appendix, net percentages in Table A.2). Our previous report documented the closing of the real gender gap in household computer access between 1989 and 1993; 1997 data indicate that, even though availability of computers at home increased by more than 50 percent from 1993 to 1997, this equal access trend remained unchanged. It should be acknowledged, however, that data related to this outcome variable—having a computer at home—do not take into account which household member instigated the purchase of the computer or makes greatest use of it. For example, usage data presented in the appendix (see Table A.3) show that men use a home computer much

---

[16]"More African Americans Plan to Go Online," *Interactive Daily,* February 18, 1997.

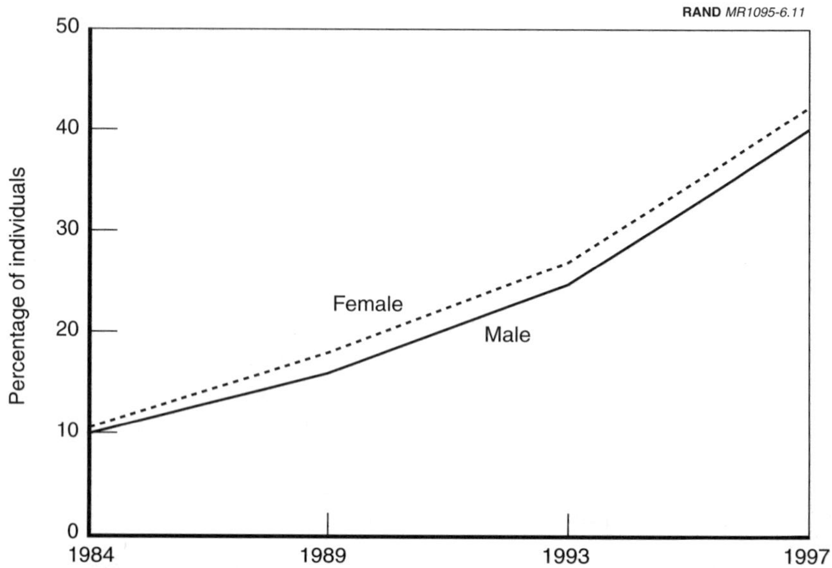

Figure 11—People in Computer Households, by Gender

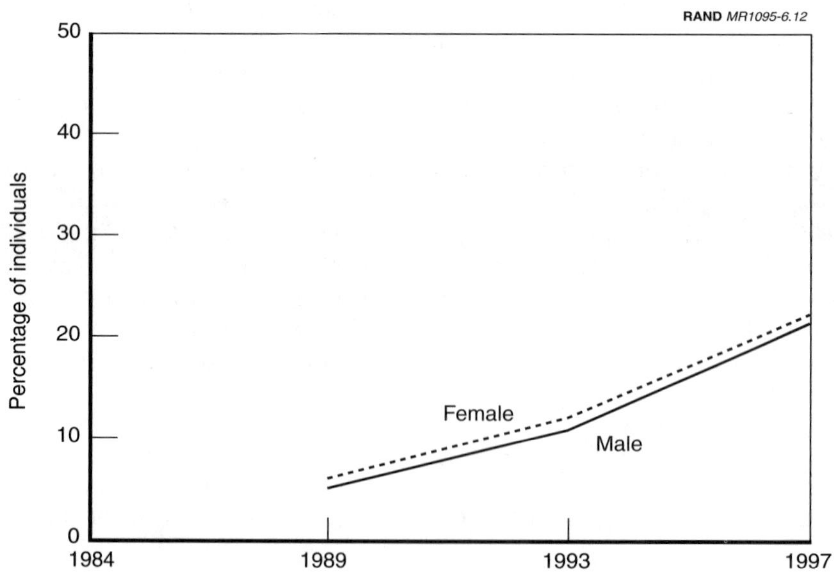

Figure 12—People Using Network Services, by Gender

more frequently than women do, even though they are approximately equally likely to be users if they have household access.

Figure 12 shows that use of network services exhibits similar variation as a function of sex when gross data are examined—a discrepancy of about 2.4 percentage points favoring male network users. When the influence of other socioeconomic variables is controlled, the size of the difference is much reduced but remains statistically significant (see the appendix, Table A.2). This latter result is surprising, because analyses of data for both 1989 and 1993 produced no statistically significant gender differences in network use when the influence of other socioeconomic variables was held constant.

That this difference in network access has persisted and widened somewhat rather than disappeared over the most recent years for which CPS data are available conflicts with the general perception, expressed in our previous report as well as other studies, that the gender gap is closing (Hoffman, Novak, and Venkatesh, 1998; Sproull, in press). Although the net growth in the access gap during this period is fairly small (from a tenth of a percent difference in 1993 to 1 percent in 1997) and may have no social policy significance, CPS data provide a more reliable representation of the U.S. population than other data sources do. We therefore recommend continued careful tracking of gender-based trends in use of digital technologies in the next CPS supplements.

Differences by location of residence. Home computer penetration and access to network services as a function of residential location, the last predictor variable we explored in detail, are shown in Figures 13 and 14. Location is categorized as rural or urban, where "urban" characterizes residences within standard metropolitan areas as the census defines them.[17]

Ostensibly, the household computer penetration rate in urban areas is much higher than in rural areas. In 1997, about 45 percent of individuals living in an urban area had a computer at home, compared with about 35 percent among rural residents (see Figure 13). About

---

[17]These areas are defined using the Office of Management and Budget's June 30, 1984, definitions.

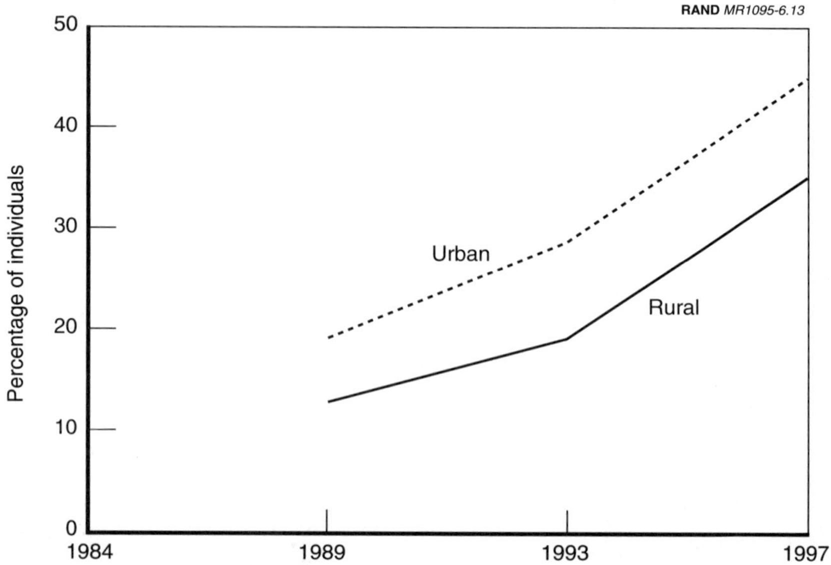

Figure 13—People in Computer Households, by Location

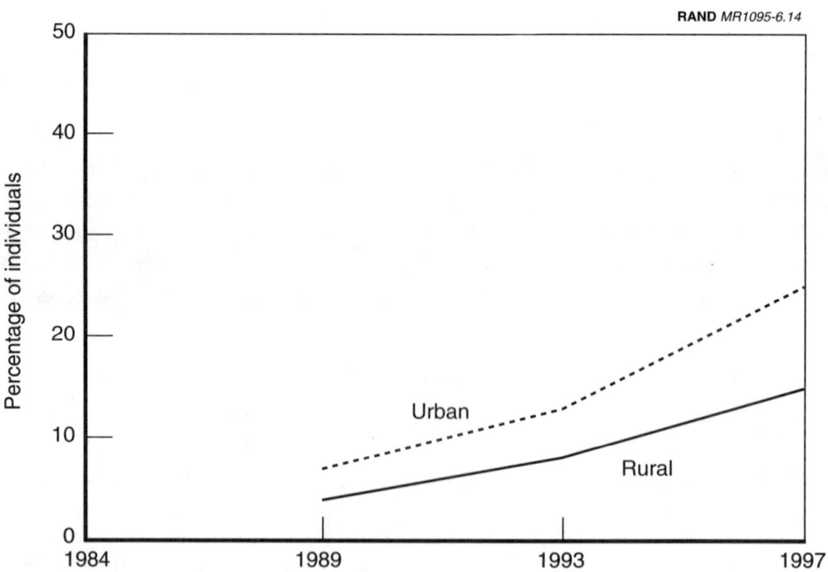

Figure 14—People Using Network Services, by Location

half of the difference is due to correlation with other characteristics, such as household income or education; nonetheless, the net gap is statistically significant. As pointed out in our earlier report, the urban-rural gap in home computer access had remained approximately constant between 1989 and 1993. Between 1993 and 1997, however, it narrowed significantly (see the appendix, Tables A.1 and A.2).

There are also substantial gross differences in people's use of network services as a function of household location. About 25 percent of residents in urban areas made use of network services in 1997, whereas the figure is 15 percent for rural residents. Again, approximately half of the difference is due to characteristics such as income and education. However, when the influence of these characteristics is held constant, the gap remains. Further, the gap between rural and urban use of network services widened significantly between 1993 and 1997 (see the appendix , Tables A.1 and A.2).

These analyses do not adequately reflect large-scale geographic variation in computers and connectivity. People living in the southeastern states, for instance, continue to lag people in all other regions in access to a computer at home (34 percent penetration rate) or to network services anywhere (18 percent penetration rate). Nor do our analyses do justice to the range of variation in digital media access to be found within particular urban or rural contexts. For instance, a study of distressed urban areas found that telephone and cable companies all too often have moved quickly to wire wealthier suburbs, bypassing poorer neighborhoods in the inner city. The lack of adequate telecommunications facilities makes problems not just for individuals but also for businesses, feeding a downward spiral in which lack of investment at the community level leads to fewer economic opportunities for the people who live there (Krieg, 1995). At the same time, unemployment, poverty, and outmigration have exacerbated the structural problems of many rural areas, according to one Office of Technology Assessment report. Today's high-technology businesses are attracted by a highly skilled work force plus network connections to other economic markets, which are what many rural areas lack (Office of Technology Assessment, 1991). Such more finely grained assessments provide an important complement to the large-scale analyses reported here.

CONCLUSIONS

Research carried out at RAND and elsewhere provides evidence that access to computers and communication networks influences opportunities to participate effectively in a range of economic, educational, social, and civic activities. The ability to interact with government agencies will soon be influenced by such technologies as well.

For these kinds of reasons, it is important to find out whether parts of the U.S. population are cut off from the emerging information society on the basis of their socioeconomic status. To address this question, our analyses sought to learn whether significant differences in access to these digital media existed in 1993 and 1997 and, if so, what had happened to the sizes of these differences over time. Table 1 serves as a score card summarizing the results we have discussed in this report.

While the score card does not present findings in numeric form, it highlights the main conclusions from detailed quantitative analyses: There is a "digital divide" between those who do and do not have access to computers and communication technologies; the division is significantly predicted by income, education, race/ethnicity, and—to a lesser extent—age, location, and possibly gender. For the most part, as Table 1 shows, these disparities have persisted over a period in which the technologies of interest have decreased dramatically in price (relative to what they can do) and increased markedly in user friendliness. More worrisome still, many of these socioeconomically based gaps have widened over this period.

These conclusions, drawn from a national sample of the U.S. population, are disturbing: Sizable demographic subgroups that remain on the wrong side of the digital divide may be deprived of the benefits associated with citizenship in an information society. In democracies, however, it is usually regarded as unfair to exclude individuals from the means for accessing information, communicating ideas, and participating in voluntary associations, civic organizations, and political activities (Anderson et al., 1995; Hochschild, 1981).

Further, as we pointed out at the beginning of this report, society as a whole loses out when broad and equitable access to these media

	Computer at Home			Use of Network Services		
	1997	1993	What Happened over Time to Gaps	1997	1993	What Happened over Time to Gaps
Income quartile						
Bottom vs. top	Yes	Yes	Widened	Yes	Yes	Constant
Bottom vs. 3rd	Yes	Yes	Widened	Yes	Yes	Constant
Bottom vs. 2nd	Yes	Yes	Constant	Yes	Yes	Narrowed
Education level						
High school vs. college	Yes	Yes	Constant	Yes	Yes	Widened
High school vs. dropout	Yes	Yes	Constant	Yes	Yes	Narrowed
Race/ethnicity						
White vs. Hispanic	Yes	Yes	Widened	Yes	Yes	Widened
White vs. black	Yes	Yes	Widened	Yes	Yes	Widened
White vs. Asian	Yes	Yes	Constant	Yes	Yes	Narrowed
White vs. Native Amer.	Yes	Yes	Narrowed	Yes	Yes	Constant
Age group						
20–39 vs. 60+	Yes	Yes	Widened	Yes	Yes	Widened
20–39 vs. 40–59	No	No	—	Yes	No	Widened
20–39 vs. 0–19	Yes	Yes	Widened	Yes	Yes	Narrowed
Sex: male vs. female	No	No		Yes	No	Widened
Location: urban vs. rural	Yes	Yes	Narrowed	Yes	Yes	Widened

Table 1

Summary of Socioeconomic Findings

is lacking. Thus, according to a recent NRC report (National Research Council, Computer Science and Telecommunications Board, 1997b, p. 30):

> As increasing fractions of the population become connected to a network, those left unconnected become an increasing burden on the democratic principle, and the cost of subsidizing their inclusion becomes smaller and smaller. Sooner or later the political calculus tips the balance toward a policy of guaranteeing universal service.

Our study of e-mail communications between government agencies and their citizen clients gives reasons for thinking that the shift should come soon, if governments are to realize the advantages of efficiency and quality potentially afforded by digital media. In 1982,

Time magazine announced the arrival of the long-envisioned "information revolution" by naming the personal computer "Machine of the Year" (Sproull, in press). Now, over a decade and a half later, we still have only half a revolution.

Appendix

ADDITIONAL INFORMATION ON CITIZENS, COMPUTERS, AND CONNECTIVITY

This appendix consists of three parts. First, we explain the procedure for computing "net" differences in home computer access and network service use, and we present a table with "gross" and "net" differences. Second, we explain our approach to statistical tests of the significance of widening or narrowing of gaps between 1993 and 1997. Third, we present additional material, not discussed in the main body of the report, on the purposes for which individuals use home computers.

NET DISPARITIES ACROSS SOCIOECONOMIC GROUPS

The focus of *Citizens, Computers, and Connectivity* is on disparities across socioeconomic groups in their access to a home computer and their use of network services. As briefly outlined in the main text, tabulations based on raw data may lead to misleading conclusions. For example, in order to assess the impact of income on the diffusion of computers, it would be misleading only to look at disparities across income groups. Part of the gap between low- and high-income families may stem from other socioeconomic characteristics, such as educational attainment. To account for the effects of all other predictor variables of interest, we employ a multivariate regression technique. The six characteristics of interest are household income, educational attainment, race and ethnicity, age, sex, and location of residence (urban or rural).

Both outcome variables, presence of a home computer and use of network services, are binary (yes/no) variables. The use of linear regression techniques, such as ordinary least squares (OLS) or analysis of variance (ANOVA), would be inappropriate, since these do not guarantee that predicted fractions are between 0 and 1. The statistical models most commonly used to estimate binary outcomes are the logistical regression (logit) and probit models. The choice between them is largely arbitrary; we opted for the logit model (Maddala, 1983).

The procedure is as follows. First, we estimate multivariate logit models to explain, say, the presence of a home computer using the six categorical predictor variables listed above. Second, to determine net disparities by, say, sex, for each individual in the sample, we predict the probability that he or she has a home computer under the counterfactual assumption that everyone is female. That is, if everyone were female, but otherwise with the same characteristics that he or she actually has, what would be the probability that each person would have a computer? Third, we average these predicted probabilities over all individuals in the sample to obtain the predicted fraction of the population that would have a computer if everyone were female. This prediction is repeated under the counterfactual assumption that everyone is male, and averaged over all individuals in the sample to obtain an estimate of the fraction having a computer among males. The resulting fractions are termed *net* fractions, as they represent differences that are due only to sex, controlling for all other socioeconomic characteristics of interest. This procedure is repeated for the other five socioeconomic predictor variables. The same procedure is used to compute net percentages of network service users.

Table A.1 shows logit coefficient estimates of 1997 presence of a home computer (column 1) and network service use (column 3). (Columns 2 and 4 are explained below.) Positive values indicate a greater propensity to have a home computer or make use of network services. The omitted category is a non-Hispanic white male age 20 to 39 who lives in a rural area and is a high school graduate (but not a college graduate) with a household income in the bottom quartile. Note that most coefficients are highly significant, in part because of the very large sample sizes (143,129 individuals in 1993 plus 123,249 in 1997).

Table A.1
Logit Estimates

	Access to Home Computer		Use of Network Services	
	1997	1993 – 1997	1997	1993 – 1997
Constant	–1.4651 ***	–1.0032 ***	–1.9056 ***	–0.8034 ***
	(0.0258)	(0.0388)	(0.0337)	(0.561)
Second income quartile	0.7279 ***	0.0055	0.5678 ***	0.2075 ***
	(0.0224)	(0.351)	(0.0315)	(0.531)
Third income quartile	1.4398 ***	–0.1316 ***	1.0508 ***	0.0693
	(0.0213)	(0.0331)	(0.0291)	(0.0500)
Top income quartile	2.2376 ***	–0.0826 *	1.6499 ***	–0.0722
	(0.0230)	(0.0341)	(0.0290)	(0.0495)
Income not reported	0.7223 ***	0.3332 ***	0.6726 ***	–0.2225 ***
	(0.0264)	(0.0429)	(0.0353)	(0.0665)
Enrolled in school	0.1532 ***	0.0925 *	–0.5237 ***	–0.6403 ***
	(0.0326)	(0.0464)	(0.0367)	(0.0777)
High school dropout	–0.5159 ***	0.0602	–1.0167 ***	–0.8207 ***
	(0.0268)	(0.0409)	(0.0413)	(0.0812)
College graduate	0.7375 ***	0.0309	1.1568 ***	–0.3008 ***
	(0.0190)	(0.0261)	(0.0192)	(0.0279)
Hispanic	–0.8745 ***	0.0941 *	–0.7029 ***	0.2389 ***
	(0.0244)	(0.0392)	(0.0329)	(0.0572)
Black	–0.9630 ***	0.2622 ***	–0.6912 ***	0.3851 ***
	(0.0231)	(0.0344)	(0.0298)	(0.0468)
Native American	–0.1609 *	–0.4800 ***	–0.3111 **	0.2625
	(0.0731)	(0.1333)	(0.0981)	(0.1767)
Asian	0.1654 ***	–0.0435	–0.3030 ***	–0.2870 ***
	(0.0344)	(0.0494)	(0.0394)	(0.0722)
Age 0–19	0.2872 ***	–0.0928 *	–0.7096 ***	–1.1899 ***
	(0.0316)	(0.0452)	(0.0364)	(0.0836)
Age 40–59	0.0104	0.0311	–0.2907 ***	0.1931 ***
	(0.0177)	(0.0249)	(0.0189)	(0.0275)
Age 60+	–1.0046 ***	0.0873 *	–1.7937 ***	0.2419 ***
	(0.0234)	(0.0349)	(0.0323)	(0.0512)
Female	0.0018	–0.0065	–0.0809 ***	0.0536 *
	(0.0133)	(0.0188)	(0.0156)	(0.0245)
Urban	0.2179 ***	0.1028 ***	0.4269 ***	–0.1379 ***
	(0.0178)	(0.0254)	(0.0225)	(0.0347)
Location missing	0.1984 ***	0.1107 ***	0.3824 **	–0.1056 *
	(0.0236)	(0.0325)	(0.0286)	(0.0433)

NOTES: Standard errors in parentheses. Significance: * = 5 percent; ** = 1 percent; *** = 0.1 percent.

We estimated similar logit equations for access to a home computer and use of network services at home or work for 1989 and 1993 and computed net rates, as explained above. For each set of predictor variables, Table A.2 shows gross and net rates of home computer penetration and use of network services.

DID DISPARITIES BECOME SMALLER OR LARGER BETWEEN 1993 AND 1997?

We want to determine whether the gaps between socioeconomic groups have widened or narrowed from 1993 to 1997. There are several alternative approaches. For example, we could measure the gap in home computer penetration as the percentage point penetration difference between two groups. For individuals in the lowest and highest income quartiles, 1993 home computer penetration was 7 and 55 percent, respectively, i.e., the gap was 48 percentage points. By 1997, these figures had risen to 15 and 75 percent, respectively, yielding a gap of 60 percentage points. According to this definition, the gap has widened. Alternatively, we could measure the gap as the duration necessary for the disadvantaged group to achieve the penetration level of the advantaged group. Let's explore this definition further.

Figure A.1 shows a stylized home computer penetration model. The penetration rate of new technologies tends to follow a logistic pattern, and we assume that home computers and network use are no exception. Any individual jumps discretely from 0 (no home computer) to 1 (home computer), but population groups as a whole tend to move along the curve from zero penetration to some asymptote, which may or may not be 100 percent. Consider individuals in the lowest income quartile who move from 7 percent in 1993 ($Q1_{93}$) to 15 percent in 1997 ($Q1_{97}$), while those in the top quartile move from 55 percent ($Q4_{93}$) to 75 percent ($Q4_{97}$). During the same time period, the percentage point gap grew from 48 to 60 percent, but did the gap really widen? The growth rate in the lower part of the curve is lower than just above the center, so equal-paced movement to the right implies a widening percentage point differential. If equal-paced growth continues, though, the shape of the curve ensures that the penetration rates will converge.

Table A.2

Gross and Net Percentages of People Who Have Access to a Home Computer and Use Network Services at Home or Work

	Home Computer						Network Services					
	1989		1993		1997		1989		1993		1997	
	Gross	Net	Gross	Net	Gross	Net	Gross	Net	Gross	Net	Gross	Net
Household income												
Bottom quartile	5.7	7.6	7.4	10.1	15.4	20.7	1.7	3.1	2.7	4.7	7.0	11.4
Second quartile	9.3	10.6	16.6	18.5	31.5	33.9	3.4	4.1	7.8	9.1	15.4	17.4
Third quartile	18.0	17.1	30.2	28.0	52.8	49.4	6.4	5.9	13.3	11.9	26.5	24.1
Top quartile	35.0	28.7	54.8	45.9	75.1	66.5	11.5	8.1	23.0	16.6	44.5	34.2
Educational attainment												
High school dropout	6.1	11.4	8.9	17.4	17.2	30.7	0.5	0.8	1.2	2.0	5.3	9.8
High school graduate	14.3	16.1	22.2	23.8	37.3	40.1	6.7	5.7	13.6	10.6	22.7	21.6
College graduate	31.9	26.5	48.7	37.3	65.7	54.5	18.3	11.4	33.8	20.2	55.8	42.4
Race and ethnicity												
Hispanic	7.7	10.3	12.4	17.3	21.8	30.0	2.4	4.2	4.8	8.4	10.0	15.8
Non-Hispanic white	20.2	19.1	30.6	28.8	48.7	46.2	6.9	6.3	13.1	11.9	26.6	24.6
Non-Hispanic black	8.2	11.1	13.3	18.3	22.0	28.5	2.9	4.3	6.3	9.5	11.8	15.9
Native American	7.5	10.5	12.9	19.1	35.3	43.0	2.8	4.8	7.5	11.5	14.0	20.4
Asian	24.1	20.0	37.4	30.9	55.9	49.4	5.2	4.1	9.7	7.6	25.6	20.5
Age category												
0-19	21.5	23.5	30.7	30.6	47.8	48.8	0.6	2.3	1.0	2.9	11.4	19.1
20-39	17.5	16.2	27.6	27.4	43.4	43.3	10.7	7.7	18.6	14.7	33.3	29.6
40-59	22.1	18.5	32.7	28.0	49.3	43.5	9.8	6.6	20.1	13.6	33.2	25.0
60+	5.5	7.7	10.5	14.7	19.7	25.6	0.9	1.1	3.5	4.0	7.4	8.6
Sex												
Male	18.9	18.1	27.9	26.9	43.7	42.4	6.4	6.1	11.8	11.5	24.0	23.3
Female	16.6	17.3	25.9	26.8	41.2	42.5	5.5	5.8	10.9	11.2	21.6	22.2
Location of residence												
Rural	13.2	15.5	19.3	22.9	34.9	39.3	3.9	4.9	7.6	9.5	15.0	18.4
Urban	19.0	18.1	29.2	27.8	44.5	43.3	6.5	6.1	12.5	11.8	25.0	23.8

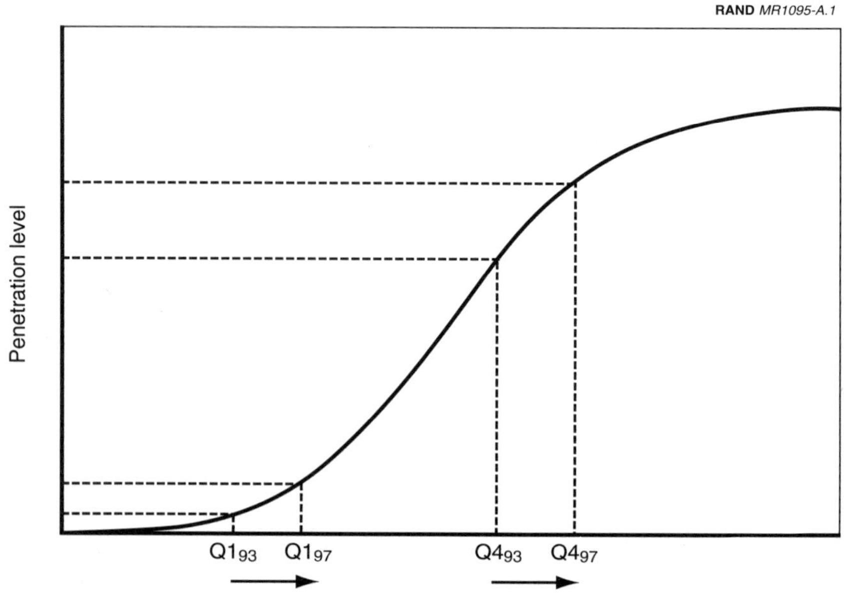

Figure A.1—Stylized Home Computer Penetration Between 1993 and 1997, by Income Quartile

Our multivariate logit models follow this penetration model. Column 1 of Table A.1 indicates that the 1997 logit-propensity to have a home computer of the top quartile exceeds that of the bottom quartile (omitted category) by 2.2376, i.e., the horizontal distance between $Q4_{97}$ and $Q1_{97}$ is 2.2376; it is significantly different from zero at 0.1 percent. We estimated the same model using 1993 data; the estimates in column 2 are the difference between 1993 and 1997 coefficient estimates.[1] In other words, estimates for 1993 are the sum of columns 1 and 2. The propensity to have a home computer in 1993 was 2.2376 – 0.0826 = 2.1550 larger for the top income quartile than for the bottom. We present the 1993 incremental (marginal) coefficients, rather than the actual coefficients, because doing so enables us to determine whether the change in the relative propensity was significant. For both home computer presence and use of network

[1]To be precise, we estimated both columns simultaneously on pooled 1993 and 1997 data, where column 1 coefficients applied to all data and column 2 to 1993 data only.

services, we find that the gap widened between 1993 and 1997. The wider gap for access to a home computer is significant at 5 percent; the increased gap for use of network services was insignificant. In either case, the gap did not widen substantially.

One way to interpret the horizontal axis is in terms of the period by which one group lags another. Note that the change in the Constant coefficient of column 2 is –1.0032, i.e., the population as a whole moved 1.0032 units to the right between 1993 and 1997. This corresponds to the population-weighted average distance between groups' positions in 1993 and 1997, i.e., the average of $Q1_{97} - Q1_{93}$, $Q4_{97} - Q4_{93}$, and so on for the other quartiles. If the population keeps moving to the right at 1.0032 units every four years, the 1993 bottom quartile may be said to lag behind the top quartile by (1997 – 1993)*2.1550/1.0032 = 8.6 years; by 1997, this lag had increased to 8.9 years. The time gap in use of network services is much shorter: At the rate of adoption experienced between 1993 and 1997, the bottom income quartile may be expected to achieve usage rates equal to those of the top income quartile in just 2.1 years. Thus interpreted, the coefficient estimates in Table A.1, columns 2 and 4, are direct measures of narrowing or widening of gaps. Table 1 on page 29 summarizes changes in gaps from 1993 to 1997 using these data. Only differences that are significant at a 5 percent confidence level or better are recorded as changes.

THE USE OF HOME COMPUTERS

We conclude with extensive tabulations of various dimensions of home computer access and use. For individuals with a home computer, Table A.3 shows the average age of the (newest) computer in years. Overall, the stock of home computers in the United States is, on average, just two years and three months old. About one out of four computerized households has more than one computer. For each individual age 3 or older living in a household with a computer, the CPS asks whether that individual uses the computer directly. Overall, 71.2 percent of those with a home computer use the computer directly.

Table A.3

Computer Use at Home (percent)

	Among Those with a Home Computer			Among Those Who Directly Use the Home Computer													
	Est. average of newest comp. (yrs)	Have more than one comp. in household	Use comp. for any purpose	Word process.	Bookkeep., finance, taxes, household records	E-mail	Desktop pub., newsletters	Games	Graphic design	Databases	Spreadsheets	Internet, other on-line service	Connect to comp. at work or school	Work at home	School assignments	Learning to use comp.	Use comp. 5+ days per week
Total	**2.24**	**24.8**	**71.2**	**60.9**	**40.0**	**35.9**	**16.7**	**62.8**	**23.4**	**24.2**	**26.5**	**42.1**	**10.2**	**31.7**	**30.1**	**20.0**	**33.4**
Sex																	
Male	2.19	26.2	72.0	57.0	42.3	39.1	16.3	66.4	24.0	27.4	30.2	47.9	12.9	35.0	28.5	19.3	37.7
Female	2.22	24.2	70.3	64.9	37.3	33.9	17.1	58.5	22.8	21.2	23.1	38.0	8.3	28.2	31.3	20.3	29.9
Age category																	
0-19	2.13	24.8	71.6	41.6	5.6	20.5	8.9	81.0	18.4	9.3	9.4	34.7	2.7	7.1	57.3	23.6	29.3
20-29	2.02	22.6	75.8	71.3	35.1	47.9	16.3	59.6	24.0	23.0	26.4	48.3	17.2	26.4	36.1	17.5	38.6
30-39	2.11	23.8	76.3	68.7	48.3	45.7	19.3	58.3	27.7	27.0	31.1	45.6	15.8	39.2	13.3	18.9	35.0
40-49	2.25	28.9	72.1	71.4	46.5	43.9	18.9	50.4	27.3	28.0	30.8	44.3	14.9	39.2	12.2	17.4	34.7
50-59	2.45	28.1	65.7	73.4	48.2	44.3	18.0	43.7	25.8	30.3	30.7	42.5	13.5	41.2	8.3	17.3	36.6
60+	2.82	21.4	54.1	68.1	49.3	36.5	13.4	46.4	20.8	24.3	24.1	33.9	5.4	22.8	3.1	17.7	39.1
Education																	
< High school	2.19	23.2	69.2	58.0	8.9	25.9	8.1	69.7	19.7	8.5	8.5	31.5	3.3	7.8	65.4	17.4	34.7
HS graduate	2.23	21.4	66.7	65.5	40.3	39.0	15.0	58.3	25.0	22.1	23.9	39.8	10.7	25.8	20.9	19.0	34.1
College grad.	2.25	31.2	82.5	79.0	49.1	52.8	21.6	46.4	27.4	32.4	36.2	51.1	20.4	47.0	15.1	16.0	39.6

Table A.3 (continued)

	Among Those with a Home Computer			Among Those Who Directly Use the Home Computer													
	Est. average of newest comp. (yrs)	Have more than one comp. in household	Use comp. for any purpose	Word process.	Bookkeep., finance, taxes, household records	E-mail	Desktop pub., newsletters	Games	Graphic design	Databases	Spreadsheets	Internet, other on-line service	Connect to comp. at work or school	Work at home	School assignments	Learning to use comp.	Use comp. 5+ days per week
Race/ethnicity																	
Hispanic	1.89	17.8	61.5	55.8	33.8	27.8	14.5	59.6	20.1	19.9	20.3	38.0	7.5	27.7	34.6	23.5	32.1
White	2.23	25.9	72.7	61.7	40.6	37.9	17.1	62.9	24.0	24.8	27.2	43.9	10.9	32.0	28.9	19.4	34.1
Black	2.13	17.5	66.5	55.6	38.7	27.0	15.1	62.5	20.5	21.0	24.6	33.7	8.8	31.0	32.9	20.9	31.2
Native Amer.	2.27	24.0	61.5	54.4	36.0	30.2	19.8	66.6	31.1	29.0	25.5	36.2	9.5	30.8	33.9	20.7	38.9
Asian	2.15	30.7	63.7	59.8	32.6	36.0	12.8	58.0	19.9	23.4	26.5	44.5	12.0	30.3	38.9	22.0	35.9
Location																	
Rural	2.34	17.7	69.6	56.0	40.1	27.6	15.4	67.5	23.5	21.1	23.0	33.8	6.5	27.0	30.2	18.1	31.4
Urban	2.16	27.1	71.3	61.8	39.9	38.5	17.0	61.5	23.5	25.2	27.7	45.1	11.7	33.6	29.4	20.5	34.7
income quartile																	
Bottom	2.13	18.7	66.5	58.8	31.7	33.5	12.8	62.8	22.2	19.4	21.6	38.2	9.7	20.0	35.9	22.1	36.6
Second	2.23	15.3	67.8	56.4	37.6	30.2	15.6	66.7	22.6	20.4	20.8	36.7	7.0	24.7	30.9	22.5	33.4
Third	2.29	20.8	70.3	57.3	40.1	33.3	16.3	65.4	23.6	23.4	25.0	40.1	8.6	29.4	28.9	20.3	32.0
Top	2.13	33.4	74.8	65.9	42.4	42.5	18.3	60.2	24.2	28.1	31.6	49.7	14.0	39.0	29.5	18.8	34.3
Employment status																	
Student	2.12	25.5	70.8	43.4	9.1	22.4	10.1	79.2	18.5	13.2	14.9	38.8	4.8	9.8	58.7	23.5	29.9
Employee	2.22	24.3	73.8	70.8	44.9	45.0	17.8	55.4	26.6	26.8	30.5	45.0	15.8	38.0	14.6	17.5	33.5
Employer	2.20	33.7	72.4	68.4	57.3	46.9	23.6	45.0	28.9	34.4	34.0	47.8	15.0	56.8	8.1	17.2	46.5
Unemployed	2.12	24.1	74.8	69.4	37.1	41.3	17.5	56.4	27.4	24.0	27.3	44.6	6.4	17.1	21.2	26.3	43.5
Other	2.36	22.7	62.3	64.8	34.5	35.9	13.1	56.6	20.6	17.3	17.1	35.7	4.6	10.6	24.8	19.2	37.2

Table A.3 (continued)

	Among Those with a Home Computer			Among Those Who Directly Use the Home Computer													
	Est. average of newest comp. (yrs)	Have more than one comp. in household	Use comp. for any purpose	Word process.	Bookkeep., finance, taxes, household records	E-mail	Desktop pub., newsletters	Games	Graphic design	Databases	Spreadsheets	Internet, other on-line service	Connect to comp. at work or school	Work at home	School assignments	Learning to use comp.	Use comp. 5+ days per week
School type																	
Public HS	2.23	23.3	88.2	60.8	3.6	25.8	8.0	71.9	20.5	7.0	7.6	30.9	2.6	5.7	79.3	18.5	35.0
Private HS	2.16	35.1	92.1	72.5	3.1	35.3	10.8	70.1	24.8	9.7	9.0	40.6	6.3	10.1	85.2	19.5	42.6
Public college	2.09	27.1	82.9	81.5	26.1	48.3	16.3	53.1	26.9	24.1	27.2	47.3	21.2	22.5	80.0	20.2	43.5
Private college	2.04	35.2	75.7	82.9	27.2	56.6	19.9	47.5	28.5	29.7	28.7	53.9	29.7	29.8	79.5	19.4	46.5
Disability status																	
Able	2.20	25.3	71.5	60.8	39.9	36.6	16.8	62.6	23.5	24.5	26.9	43.3	10.7	31.9	30.2	19.8	33.9
Disabled	2.31	22.8	57.9	64.9	36.0	33.2	12.4	58.1	22.8	19.5	19.6	34.5	7.9	22.9	13.8	20.3	34.8
Region																	
Northeast	2.26	23.3	69.6	58.5	36.6	36.2	14.9	60.1	20.5	23.0	23.2	43.9	10.2	30.8	29.9	20.3	32.7
Midwest	2.24	23.6	71.6	59.3	39.8	34.1	16.4	65.1	23.3	23.7	26.9	41.0	10.4	30.8	31.0	19.9	30.8
South	2.15	25.0	71.5	59.5	41.0	36.8	15.9	63.3	22.6	24.0	26.5	43.6	10.4	31.6	28.0	17.4	35.7
West	2.19	28.4	71.5	65.8	40.8	39.0	19.1	61.0	26.8	26.4	29.4	43.7	11.5	33.3	31.2	22.2	35.5

For those who use a computer at home, the CPS then asks how often and for what purposes the individual uses the computer. The most common use, at 62.8 percent, is to play games, followed closely by word processing. Other popular uses are bookkeeping or keeping track of finances, taxes, or household records; connecting to the Internet; sending e-mail; working at home; and doing school assignments. Home computers appear to be used quite intensively: about one out of three home computer users reports using it at least five days per week. Three out of four use it at least two days per week (not shown in the table).

REFERENCES

Anderson, Robert H., Tora K. Bikson, Sally Ann Law, and Bridger M. Mitchell (1995). *Universal Access to E-Mail: Feasibility and Societal Implications*, Santa Monica, CA: RAND, MR-650-MF.

The Benton Foundation (1998). "Defining the Technology Gap," *Losing Ground Bit by Bit: Low Income Communities in the Information Age*, Washington, D.C.: The Benton Foundation, pp. 1–8.

Educational Testing Service (1997). *Computers and Classrooms: The Status of Technology in U.S. Schools*, Princeton, NJ: Educational Testing Service.

Firestone, Charles, and Amy Korzick Garner (1998). Foreword to *Investing in Diversity*, Washington, D.C.: The Aspen Institute, pp. v–xi.

Hochschild, Jennifer L. (1981). *What's Fair: American Beliefs About Distributive Justice*, Boston: Harvard University Press.

Hoffman, D. L., W. Kalsbeek, and T. P. Novak (1996). "Internet and Web Use in the United States: Baseline for Commercial Development," *Communications of the ACM*, 39(12) (December), pp. 36–46.

Hoffman, D. L., and T. P. Novak (1998). "Bridging the Racial Divide on the Internet," *Science*, 280 (17 April), pp. 390–391.

Hoffman, D. L., T. P. Novak, and Alladi Venkatesh (1998). "Diversity on the Internet: The Relationship of Race to Access and Usage," *Investing in Diversity*, Washington, D.C.: The Aspen Institute.

Katz, James E., and Philip Aspden (1996). "Motivations for and Barriers to Internet Usage: Results of a National Public Opinion Survey," paper presented at 24th Annual Telecommunications Policy Research Conference, Solomons, MD (October).

Kraut, Robert, et al. (1996). "The HomeNet Field Trial of Residential Internet Services," *Communications of the ACM*, 39(12) (December), pp. 55–63.

Kreuger, Alan (1993). "How Computers Have Changed the Wage Structure: Evidence from Microdata, 1984–1989," *Quarterly Journal of Economics*, 108, pp. 33–60.

Krieg, Richard (1995). "Information Technology and Low-Income, Inner City Communities," *Journal of Urban Technology*, 3(1), pp. 1–17.

National Partnership for Reinventing Government (1993). *Access America: Reengineering Government Through Information Technology*, Washington, D.C.: U.S. Government Printing Office. Also available at http://www.npr/gov/library/reports/it.html.

National Research Council, Computer Science and Telecommunications Board (1997a). *More Than Screen Deep: Toward Every-Citizen Interfaces to the Nation's Information Infrastructure*, Washington, D.C.: National Academy Press.

National Research Council, Computer Science and Telecommunications Board (1997b). *Fostering Research on the Economic and Social Impacts of Information Technology*, Washington, D.C.: National Academy Press.

National Telecommunications and Information Administration (1998). *Falling Through the Net II: New Data on the Digital Divide*, Washington, D.C.: U.S. Government Printing Office.

Office of Technology Assessment (1991). *Rural America at the Crossroads: Networking for the Future*, Washington, D.C.: U.S. Government Printing Office.

Schofield, J. W. (1995). *Computers, Classroom Culture, and Change,* Cambridge, UK: Cambridge University Press.

Schofield, J. W., and A. L. Davidson (1997). "The Internet in School: The Shaping of Use by Organizational, Structural, and Cultural Factors," in S. Lobodzinski and I. Tomek (eds.), *Proceedings of WebNet 97—World Conference of the WWW, Internet & Intranet,* Charlottesville, VA: Association for the Advancement of Computing in Education, pp. 485–489.

Sproull, Lee (in press). "Computers in the U.S. Household: 1977–1997," in Alfred D. Chandler, Jr., and James W. Cortada (eds.), *The Information Age in Historical Perspective: The Role of Information in the Transformation of the United States from Colonial Times to the Present,* New York: Oxford University Press.

U.S. Bureau of the Census (1985). *Current Population Survey,* October 1984, Washington, D. C.: U.S. Bureau of the Census.

U.S. Bureau of the Census (1990). *Current Population Survey,* October 1989, Washington, D.C.: U.S. Bureau of the Census.

U.S. Bureau of the Census (1994). *Current Population Survey,* October 1993, Washington, D.C.: U.S. Bureau of the Census.

U.S. Bureau of the Census (1998). *Current Population Survey,* October 1997, Washington, D.C.: U.S. Bureau of the Census.

Wilhelm, Anthony (1998). *Closing the Digital Divide: Enhancing Hispanic Participation in the Information Age,* Claremont, CA: The Tomas Rivera Policy Institute.